I Can Read It

Word Lists

By John Holzmann
Decorated by Drew Thurston

Published by
Sonlight Curriculum, Ltd.
8042 South Grant Way
Littleton, CO 80122-2705
(303) 730-6292 FAX (303) 795-8668
E-Mail: main@sonlight.com

For HELP: www.sonlight-forums.com/langart

ISBN 1-887840-46-X

Preface

We had several goals in mind as we put this book together.

1. To provide a thorough, low-cost, phonetically-correct introduction to reading.

By "phonetically-correct" I mean we have consistently and deliberately sought—to the best of our ability—to present words within phonetic patterns. And we highlight those patterns.

Note: We also use "sight" words—words your child must memorize. But we have attempted to keep these words to a minimum and to maintain our focus on the phonetic patterns.

2. To provide a program that *includes* phonetically-correct *reading* materials to go along with the phonics lessons themselves.

If you have looked at the reading instruction marketplace, you have probably noted that there are few if any phonetically-correct programs that are both low-cost and include reading materials. You can get low-cost phonetically-correct programs that don't include reading materials. Or you can acquire phonetically-correct programs with reading materials that are relatively high-priced (in the $200-plus range). We wanted to produce a program that included both the reading materials and the low price.

3. To provide readings that have a relatively high level of interest to students. In other words, to provide real stories, complete with conflict, action, and plot.

This, too, we believe, is rare. We do not wish to suggest that ours are either "the best," or the only "good" phonetically-correct stories on the market. However, it has been our observation that the best stories pay little attention to phonics/phonetics, and those readers that are phonetically correct tend to feature stories that are—what shall we say?—not exactly enticing! They seem to lack the plot and conflict that fulfill vital functions in all "real" stories, the "best" stories.

We wanted to overcome this deficiency.

Finally, we wanted

4. To provide enough reading material so that average students will neither grow bored nor be pushed so fast that they feel

inadequate for the task they are being asked to do. Above all, **we don't want kids to quit in frustration.**

A goal that we did not hold in too high regard:

We did not think that we had to maintain absolutely perfect standards when it came to tense and some other finer points of grammar. As a result, I have sometimes chosen phonetic consistency over grammatical consistency. Thus you will find "Nat the cat *sat* on a mat" (past tense) and, in the very next sentence, he "*is*" on the same mat (present). Then, just as suddenly (next sentence), he is back in the past as he "*sat* on a hat on the mat."

Why did I do this? Because, for example, beginning readers may be able to read "he sat'" (past tense) and "he is" (present tense) but they have not yet studied "sits" (present tense) or "was," (past tense). Similarly, early readers learn the short *e* form of the past tense verb *met* ("he met") long before they learn the long *e* form of the present-tense verb *meet* or *meets*.

Please understand: I am directing your attention to these matters.

I would guess that, without my cluing you in, most readers would miss the fact that our stories contain these "flaws." But for the sake of the few who do notice such things—and for whom correct grammar is exceedingly important (I count myself among you!)—I wanted you to know my intentions. I wanted you to understand some of the deliberative thinking that went into developing this book. And so I am here revealing my "secrets"!

We thought it would be better to give students interesting stories that occasionally bent the rules of grammar than to slavishly obey the rules of grammar and, thereby, narrow the scope of students' readings to inane or disconnected sentences.

You would think that writing stories with limited vocabulary would be a piece of cake. Not so!

This has been, to my mind, the most difficult project I have ever undertaken.

I spent more than two months on this project full time. And that's not including the time I spent gathering information and laying down the "rules" and principles we would follow. Nor does it include the editing, revising, and typesetting that followed.

As an author, I am used to being able to utilize whatever words come to mind. But in this case, I was required to limit myself—especially in the very earliest sections—to an exceptionally narrow range of words. I would have an idea in mind, I could express it in any of 100 ways if I were permitted to use my normal vocabulary, but, after thoroughly testing every permutation and combination imaginable, I would find myself forced to the conclusion that *that* particular concept, *that* action, *that* outcome, was *impossible*. The man, rat, cat, or whatever or whoever it was that I was dealing with: he or she simply could not be made to do what I had in mind. So I would look for another plot twist.

When I first started the project, I found I could handle no more than five minutes of this mental torture at a time. Often, half an hour of work would put me under the table, asleep. My mind would simply shut off!

My highest regards to all the authors who have preceded me in writing phonetically correct readers. . . . My thanks, too, to my wife, Sarita (Sunbeam!) and all the staff at Sonlight Curriculum who, despite my moaning and groaning, permitted and encouraged me to finish this task. And, last but not least, thanks to Mary Elizabeth Hall who graciously helped me rework some of the knottier stories from the first edition and Suzanne Hamrick who provided invaluable recommendations concerning how to teach.

May God bless you as you train your children in the way they should go!

John Holzmann
Highlands Ranch, CO
27 February 2002 (Revised 21 May 2004)

Table of Contents

How to Teach Kids How to Read

An Overview

The ability to read comes as a result of several analytic and synthetic skills: abilities to pull language apart and to put it back together.

If we think of spoken language as the most "natural" form of language, then we can see that writers have to translate speech into writing. In English, that means they have to break their thoughts into individual words and their words into letters. At this point, the idea is so "natural" to you, you can hardly imagine all the difficulties entailed.

So let's look at the other end of the equation. Let's think of what is required in order to synthesize speech again from writing, since that's what we are hoping to enable your children to do.

When you teach your children to read, you will help impart at least the following knowledge and/or skills. You will teach them:

1. That words are made of separate sounds. The word *cat*, for instance, is made of the sounds /k/, /a/, and /t/. *Bad* is composed of /b/, /a/, and /d/.
2. That letters of the alphabet are meant to communicate certain sounds.
3. What specific sounds each letter makes (the "rules of phonics").
4. How to blend those sounds together to form the same kinds of sounds one hears when one listens to normal speech. (The letters *cat*, when put together as I have just done—with no spaces between, yet with spaces (and/or punctuation marks) surrounding them— . . . The letters *cat* don't spell /k/ . . . /a/ . . . /t/—all drawn out and voiced in three discrete time frames. Rather, they spell the word we pronounce /kat/.)
5. How to string these words together and inflect their voices meaningfully . . . in order to form meaningful (or meaningful *sounding*) sentences.
6. To *recognize* the words they are forming and to *understand* their meanings.
7. To understand the meanings of the sentences they are forming. . . . And so forth.

These different skills I've just outlined parallel a "normal" progression in how children learn to read.

Most children begin to read using a **phonics-decoding method**. It is common for children in kindergarten and first grade to learn to recognize letters, letter-combinations, and the standard sounds for which they stand.

By second or third grade, most children have moved on to **fluency** in reading. At fluency, decoding becomes a relative non-issue. Children who are fluent readers tend to recognize words in print much the way they recognize words when spoken: they process the words without having to think about it. Phonics practice at this stage is useful primarily as a spelling aid.

Finally, at about the fourth grade (again, we are speaking "on average"!), children move on to reading for **information**. At this stage, most children are able to stop focusing so much on the words themselves and pay closer attention to the larger ideas and concepts that the words are meant to convey.

Of course, even at the phonics-decoding level, some limited amount of information ought to be getting through; and at the information stage, there are times when readers need their phonics-decoding ability in order to figure out unfamiliar words.

My point, however, is that there is a "normal" developmental progression. If you keep that progression in mind and determine to work *with* it, you will almost certainly interact more compassionately and understandingly with your children than if you demand behavior that is inappropriate to the stages where your children find themselves.

You will understand that when your children are exerting every ounce of effort on basic phonics-decoding, they can't possibly keep in mind the *stories* they are attempting to read. Indeed, in the beginning, they may need to read a single line of text two or three times before they can make it sound like natural language—much less be able to understand what that line means.

How to Use This Book

Word Lists

When we were teaching our children to read, we would read out loud with them the word lists found here in Volume 4 of *I Can Read It!* Depending on the child, we might read only two or three words in a list, then have the child read the remainder. Or we would read more words together (both parent and child reading the same word). Or we would alternate words: parent reading one, child reading the next. Or we would permit the student simply to prove his proficiency with a few words, then move on to "the heart of the matter," the story itself.

Our purpose was never simply to certify that the child had completed a lesson: "Yep, I've done it!" The point was to make sure the child was beginning to memorize and instantly recognize what s/he was seeing on the page. Put another way: we were aiming to help our children *read fluently*.

If it takes 100 repetitions of reading the same list of words before your child is able to recognize a word instantaneously, then so be it! Fluency:

that is the goal. The goal is *not* to be able to say, "*My* child finished the
_____ phonics program in 12 weeks! [What did *yours* do?]"

You will notice we have organized the words in matrices: same end-
ings combined with different initial consonants (or vice versa). Take a
look at the matrices on pages 17 and 18 for examples.

We wanted to make sure our students recognized these patterns. "The
English language is regular; it follows patterns!"

After reading whatever portion(s) of the word lists we thought would
help each child master the patterns, we would move on to the stories.

NOTE: Do not over-emphasize patterns. Children need to recognize
them. But they gain mastery of recognition through actual reading in context: seeing words that follow *different* patterns and being able to distinguish them.

So there is a balance. Your children need to see the patterns, but they
have to be able to distinguish the patterns as well. And the only way they
will learn to distinguish the patterns is by reading real words in context.

And that brings me to another point.

Every word in the lists we use is a real word. Every word can be
found in a dictionary. But some of the words are rather obscure.

If your children don't know what it means to *tat*; or if they don't recognize what a *frock* or *spud* is: we leave it to you to decide whether the
cultural literacy lesson should take precedence over the basic decoding
you're trying to teach.

It is our opinion that, in the midst of word lists that have no meaning
other than to demonstrate phonetic regularities, it probably won't hurt if
you let your children think a word has no meaning. Focus more on meaning when you get to the stories themselves.

Stories

If your children are able to read the stories on their own, that's great!
Let them. On the other hand, most children will benefit from more of a
"team" approach to reading, at least for the first couple of years.

For some, it is helpful if you "take turns" reading. You read a sentence or paragraph, then they read the next one—back and forth throughout the story. Or perhaps you don't trade off, but you have your child read
a sentence, paragraph or story and then you *reread* it.

It is quite likely, especially at the beginning of your adventure together, that your children will stumble and struggle, miss the appropriate paus-
es and emphases that they should provide based on the periods and other
ending punctuation. They will probably even forget the meaning of the
first few words of a sentence before they get to the end.

So the purpose of your re-reading is to convey to your children the
meaning and excitement of what they are laboring so mightily merely to

sound out. You want to help your children—especially at the front end of this adventure—to know that they are achieving great success simply by *focusing on decoding the sounds.* You don't want them to have to worry about "missing" punctuations, poor intonation and inflection, or missed meanings. There will be plenty of time for these things later. "You're doing great! You have gotten all the *sounds!* One of these days, not too long from now, you will be reading just like Mommy and Daddy . . ."

As you reread, slide your finger along, pointing to the letters, words and punctuation marks you are noticing and that give you clues concerning how you are supposed to read. Demonstrate *where you are looking* as you read. (For example—this is something you'd do a bit later in your reading together—point to the question mark or exclamation point, and comment on the clue it gives you for how to read the sentence: the kind of intonation you will provide.)

Besides letting your children read completely on their own or you and your children taking a tag-team approach, a third method you might like is for you to read the passage once out loud while pointing to the words and punctuation marks you are reading as you read them. (Of course, you will read with expressiveness, excitement and meaning.)

But then, after you have read the sentence, paragraph, or story, you will have your *children* read it.

If necessary, you may want to go back a third time and reread a portion of what the two of you have read.

It's Like Learning to Swim

I am reminded of how our children first learned to swim.

When they first entered the water, even though they knew the *theoretical* techniques for propelling themselves through the water, they did not have good muscle control. They spluttered and splashed and gasped for air!

And it was *okay*.

We told them what a great job they were doing. And they *were* doing a great job. Of course, they weren't swimming the way we hoped they one day would be able to swim, but they were swimming astonishingly well for first-timers!

And so we had them swim: poor style, splash, gasps, and all.

We would demonstrate over and over how they *ought* to look if and when they became really proficient. We would point out how and where and why they could improve. But mostly, we had them swim.

And over the weeks their strokes improved. They smoothed out. They stopped gasping. They calmed down. They became more efficient.

So it is with reading.

What we have tried to provide in the *I Can Read It!* books—and what we have not found elsewhere—is reading exercises and stories that will provide enough variety and interest to help motivate your children to *keep* practicing, *keep* trying. We have attempted to provide an *intrinsic reward* in the readings themselves. The stories are generally *interesting*: something we have not found elsewhere.

Yes, when you have read about Nat and Pat ten times, the story will likely lose some of its shine. But you and your children will know that the story itself *was* worth reading. It did (and does) contain a punch line. (Oh! Excuse the pun!)

But Isn't There a Point Where Repetition Can Become Harmful?

"All right," you may say. "I will read alongside my children. Maybe I will read first, maybe I will read second. But if I read to my children first, and/or if I permit them to keep rereading the same story over and over, won't they end up *memorizing* the text? And if they do that, they won't be *reading* the text; they will merely *sound* as if they are reading. And *what good will that do?*"

It is a fair question. And I have two answers.

1. The exercises and stories in this book are complex enough, we think it is extremely unlikely that your children will be able to memorize any passage even after two or three readings. By the time they have read these pieces often enough to memorize them, they will have read them more than enough to get the kind of practice in *reading* that we intend for them to get.
2. There are benefits to knowing a passage so well that it is virtually memorized. For one, when you get to know a passage that well, you can pay full attention to meanings, and inflections and intonations. If you would like your children to read out loud in an *excellent* manner, such memorization may be a great *boon!*

Some Pointers

Keep it Fun and Do-able

Above all, we want reading to be a fun pursuit. It is work. It may be very hard work. But it ought to be fun, exciting, *interesting*: because the *goal* is interesting.

As with physical exercise, if the work is too hard, you need to give your children breaks and come back to it later in the day. For many children, two or three ten-minute sessions may be far more valuable (and less stressful) than one twenty- or thirty-minute practice.

We have designed our reading program to match the needs of that nebulous "average child." As I have said elsewhere, so I will say again: **Pay attention to each of your children's personal needs and don't**

worry about how "other children" are doing! This is one reason we homeschool: because we want our kids to achieve the success that they can achieve *at their own pace*, without having to compare themselves, either favorably or unfavorably, with others.

If you find your children are chomping at the bit to read more than we have assigned, let them! Some children pick up the skill more rapidly than others.

If you find your children are struggling to keep up with the reading assignments we have made, relax! Some children simply need more practice than others. So give them the time to practice.

Probably the most important ingredient necessary to create lifelong readers is to keep them encouraged.

"Sight" Words

Throughout this book, we place "sight" words in a box whenever we first introduce them. By "sight" words I mean words that do not follow a pattern we have already studied. The words may legitimately follow a pattern (sometimes I have included a whole series of sight words that follow a pattern) but we simply don't expect students to master (or to have mastered) the pattern yet.

We highlight "sight" words that we use in a story at the bottom of each page. You will find new words highlighted in **bold**. We repeat a sight word ten times before replacing it in these lists with a new word.

If your son or daughter is unable to decode a particular blend, don't "punish," him by ridicule or harsh remarks; simply provide the sound(s) yourself and move on. . . .

We recommend that you put new sight words on index cards and drill your children with them before beginning to read for the day.

Book Pages Can Be Distracting

It is more difficult to read books than it is to read individual words. Book readers have to remember to read whole strings of words from left to right. And they have to keep their place on each line of text.

To aid your very early beginning readers, we recommend that you point to each word with your finger, a pencil, or some other pointed object. Indeed, for a time, you will probably want to point to each and every letter in order to encourage your children to make the specific sounds.

Many children, even with physical pointers helping to show the way, find it hard to concentrate when there are so many other letters on the page. They just can't get their eyes to focus on the one spot. They want to look around at everything else on the page.

If your children struggle with that kind of distraction, you may want to use a large card with an L-shaped notch cut out of the top to cover all the text to the left and below where your children happen to be reading. Or (another possible help) cut a small rectangular window in the middle of a card or sheet of paper so your children will have no distractions at all on the page. They will have nowhere else to look but inside the "window."

At first, have your children say the separate sounds of the letters and then the word as a whole. If they have difficulty, have them say (or you say with them) the sounds of the first two letters, together, and then the ending. If they don't recognize the words when they sound them out, you should say the sounds yourself slowly…and then repeat them faster.

When your children come across words that give them difficulty, help them strategize how to "sound it out." Point at or otherwise narrow their focus to individual letters or letter combinations. Verbalize the individual sounds out of which the words are formed. Or, sometimes, simply provide the word so they can keep on moving.

Some children require almost no help at all. And with a logical, carefully controlled reading text, as we have attempted to provide in these volumes, some children will progress rapidly—so rapidly you may think they are missing something.

Yet as Dr. Beechick told me: "If children can read beyond the scope of their formal phonics training, set them free." Have them read word lists and phonetic rules for the sake, perhaps, of learning how to spell accurately. But let them read what they are capable of and don't worry that they haven't completed a set number of phonics lessons.

Having just said this, however, please recognize: **a majority of children will need some coaching and sit-beside-me help**. These will benefit from the finger pointing or other aids I have described. They will also benefit from the organized word lists we have included in each lesson.

Letter Names *v* Letter Sounds

When learning to read, children need to know the letters' sounds; they don't need to know, nor do they need to use, the letters' names. So concentrate on the sounds while you're teaching your children to read. (This advice does *not* mean you should ignore the letters' names while you are teaching other skills. I am merely saying that, during the first stages of teaching children how to read, you ought not to burden them with that one additional fact. They don't need to *say* that the name of the letter *f* is pronounced /eff/. They need to know that when they see the letter *f* in print, it makes the /f/ sound.)

Children learn sounds faster in the context of words. So as soon as they know enough letters to form a few words, have your children read real three-letter words (as we do in *I Can Read It!*).

Besides using phonics workbooks and the *I Can Read It!* series, you will probably find it very helpful to have your children make words using movable letters—like the brightly-colored magnetized plastic letters you put on refrigerator doors. Or make your own movable letters by writing them on poster board and cutting them apart.

Have your children say the sounds (not the names) of all the letters as they put the characters together to form words. If you want, have your son or daughter match the words to pictures—as you may see in the Explode the Code series. Or have your children say the sounds as they trace or write the letters.

About Phonics

"English is unlike Chinese," say the advocates of phonics reading programs. "An alphabetic writing system such as ours, with its 26 letters, has significant advantages over an ideographic or pictographic system in which one has to memorize thousands of symbols in order to write thousands of words."

And this is true. English is full of regularities. And if we emphasize them, children learn to read quickly and confidently.

As I worked on this book, I spoke with Dr. Ruth Beechick, a professional educator who has provided wonderful service to the homeschool movement. Dr. Beechick underlined the importance of learning the few basic rules. "After that, the most important thing is to read, read, read! Don't worry about unfamiliar words. Most children can figure them out. Have the children read to themselves, read to their parents, read to visitors, read to Grandma. . . . "

Dr. Beechick made another observation which she repeated several times: **Don't get bogged down in phonics.**

Phonics is designed to help us read fluently and spell accurately. Keep the goal in mind. Don't make it a "subject" in its own right that must be "mastered" apart from the goal!

The bottom line: **teach your children basic phonics/phonetics, but teach them to look at the context around a word to help figure out its sound and meaning.** Thus, even if they believe the rules of phonics suggest that the word *tongue* should be pronounced /tawn-gyoo/, you need to teach them to look at the context. "The dog stuck out its tongue" more likely means he stuck out his /tung/ than that he stuck out a /tawngyoo/ (whatever that may be!).

Need Help?

Please feel free to visit www.sonlight-forums.com/langart. There are dozens of other parent-teachers just like you who have struggled with the issues you face. They will be happy to interact with you and share their strategies and war stories!

Lesson 1[1]

Three-letter words ending in -*at*

-at

bat	cat	fat	hat
mat	Matt[2]	Nat	pat
Pat	rat	sat	tat
vat			

---

[1] Basic instructions for this and all subsequent lessons can be found on pp. viii-xiii.

[2] A doubled consonant normally makes the same sound as that consonant when it appears by itself. That is certainly the case here!

Lesson 2[1]

Short *a* words ending in *n, d, m, p,* and *nd*

-an	Ann[2]	ban	can	Dan
	fan	Jan	man	Nan
	pan	ran	tan	van
-ad	bad	dad	fad	had
	lad	mad	pad	sad
	Tad			
-and	and	band	hand	land
	sand			
-am	bam	Cam	dam	ham
	jam	Pam	ram	Sam
	yam			
-ap	cap	gap	lap	map
	nap	rap	sap	tap
	yap	zap		
-as	as	has		

---

[1] You can increase the difficulty of this page by having your children read *down* the columns and not just across the rows. Notice how such an exercise forces them to pay attention to the ending sounds *as well as* the beginning letters.

[2] Again we have a double consonant. It makes the same sound as a single consonant. Also, review the fact that all proper names must be capitalized. Have your child point to the proper names on this page (Ann, Dan, Jan, Nan, Tad, Cam, Pam, Sam).

Lesson 3

Short *a* words ending in *b, g, l, s, x, z*; and words ending in
-ps and *-ts*

-ab	cab	dab	gab	jab
	lab	nab	tab	
-ag	bag	gag	hag	lag
	nag	rag	sag	tag
	wag			
-al	Al	Cal	gal	Hal
	pal	Sal	Val	
-ass	gas	lass	mass	pass
-ax	ax	fax	lax	Max
	sax	tax	wax	
-azz	jazz	razz		

Lesson 4[1]
Short *i* words plus a few *qu-* words

-ib	bib	fib	rib	
-id	bid	did	hid	kid
	lid	rid	Sid	
-if	Biff	if	riff	tiff
-ig	big	dig	fig	gig
	jig	pig	rig	wig
-ill	bill	dill	fill	gill
	hill	ill	Jill	kill
	Lil	mill	pill	quill[3]
	sill	till	will	
-im	dim	him	Jim	rim
	Tim			
-in	bin	din	fin	kin
	pin	sin	tin	thin
	win			

---

[1]You will want to remind (or teach) your child that *q* in the English language is always followed by *u* (you don't find a *q* by itself), and in almost all cases the two letters together make a /kw/ sound. Notice that we see this pattern here with *quill* and *quilt*, but also later with *quip* and *quit*. **Teaching hint:** Until your children learn to read them easily, it is usually helpful to underline two-letter combinations that make unique sounds—combinations like like *qu* and *th*.

-ip	dip	hip	lip	nip
	quip	rip	sip	tip
	yip	zip		
-iss	hiss	kiss	miss	this
-it	bit	fit	hit	kit
	lit	mitt	pit	quit
	sit	wit	it	
-ix	fix	mix	nix	six

Lesson 5
Words ending with a vocalized *s* (the *s* sounds like /z/)[1]

-ans	cans	fans	pans	vans
-ads	dads	fads	lads	pads
-ams	hams	jams	rams	yams
-ands	bands	hands	lands	sands
-ags	bags	gags	lags	nags
	rags	sags	tags	wags
-abs	gabs	jabs	nabs	tabs
-als	Al's	Cal's	gals	Hal's
	pals	Sal's	Val's	
-ibs	bibs	dibs	fibs	ribs
-ids	bids	kids	lids	rids
-igs	digs	figs	pigs	wigs
-ills	bills	fills	hills	kills

---

[1] We have actually dealt with the vocalized *s* since Lesson 1 (the words *has, is* and *his* contain vocalized *s*'s). But since *has, is* and *his* were "sight" words, your child may not have paid much attention to what was going on: some *s*'s make an unvocalized *s* sound (/s/) and others make a vocalized *s* sound (/z/; place your fingertips on the front of your neck and feel how your vocal chords vibrate when you say /z/; they don't vibrate when you say /s/)!

If you think about the way we vocalize our sounds, you will realize there is a good reason words that end in *-ns, -ds, -ms,* and so forth have vocalized *s*'s—just as there are good reasons why words that end in *-ts, -ps, -ks,* and so forth have unvocalized *s*'s. —Can you figure it out?

To learn more, turn to the back of this book, Appendix 1: Linguistics and Sound Formation. The discussion there may help you explain to your child why the "final *s*" means the same thing even if it sounds different.

	mills	pills	quills	tills
-ims	Jim's	Kim's	rims	Tim's
-ins	bins	fins	pins	sins
	tins	wins		

Lesson 6[1]
Short *u* words, including their plural forms

-ub	cub	hub	nub	pub
	rub	sub	tub	
-ug	bug	dug	hug	jug
	lug	mug	pug	rug
	tug			
-um	bum	gum	hum	mum
	rum	sum	yum	
-un	bun	fun	gun	Hun
	nun	pun	run	sun
-up	cup	pup	sup	up
-uss	bus	fuss	muss	Russ
-ut	but	cut	gut	hut
	mutt	nut	putt	rut

---

[1] As we suggested in Lesson 2, you can increase the difficulty of this page by having your children read *down* the columns and not just across the rows. Notice how such an exercise forces them to pay attention to the ending sounds *as well as* the begining letters. You can suggest that your children may ask you to take over if they get tired. After Mom or Dad has read several words, perhaps then you can switch off again . . . or read together.

Lesson 7
Plurals and present tenses of words ending in *s* and *x*

-ud	Bud	bud	cud	mud
-uff	cuff	fluff	muff	puff
-uzz	buzz	fuzz		
-axes[1]	axes	faxes	taxes	waxes
-ixes	fixes	mixes	sixes	
-asses	lasses	masses	passes	sasses
-isses	hisses	kisses	misses	
-x's	fax's	Max's	tax's	mix's

.

---

[1] Notice that each of these words has a second part (*-es*: *ax-es*; *fax-es*; *tax-es*; and so forth). They need the *es* ending because it is too difficult to say *axs* or *faxs*. Our voices and ears need the "space" of the /e/ sound in order to be able to distinguish the sound of the final *s*.

Lesson 8

Short *e* words, plus the soft forms of *c* and *g*[1]

-ed	bed	fed	led	Ned
	red	Ted	wed	
-eg	beg	egg[2]	leg	peg
-ell	bell	cell	dell	fell
	hell	Nell	quell	sell
	tell	well	yell	
-em	gem	hem	Lem	them
-en	Ben	den	hen	Jen
	Ken	men	pen	ten
	then	when	yen	
-end	bend	lend	mend	send
-ep	pep	yep	step	
-ess	Bess	bless	dress	Jess

---

[1] Just as the letter *s* can make two sounds, so, too, the letters *c* and *g* make two different sounds Both of these consonants have what linguists call "hard" and "soft" sounds, and they make these hard and soft sounds depending on what vowels follow them. The letter *c*, for example, has a hard /k/ sound when it is followed by *a*, *o*, or *u*. It has a soft /s/ sound if it is followed by *e*, *i*, or (when we get to it) the vowel form of *y*. For example, we find the hard *c* in the words *cat, cot* and *cut*, but the soft *c* in *cell, cinder* and *cycle*.

[2] The letter *g* is not quite as regular as the letter *c*. It is always hard when followed by *a, o* or *u* (*gander, go, gut*). It is almost always soft when followed by *e, i*, or *y* (*gel* and *gem* but not *get*), *gin* (not *giddy*) and *gyroscope* (not *gynecology*)).

	less	mess	press	stress
-et	bet	get	jet	let
	met	net	pet	set
	vet	wet	yet	
-ex	Rex	Tex	vex	

Lesson 9

Review. . . with emphasis on reading speed and accuracy[1]

-ex's Rex's Tex's

-exes sexes vexes

-esses blesses dresses messes presses

stresses tresses

---

[1] Feel free either to briefly explain the meanings of the unfamiliar words or simply encourage your that they will learn what the words mean as they read stories. "Look at the whole word. Try to say it. If unsure, try to say the first two sounds and then the ending. Can you figure it out?"

Lesson 10
Short *o* words

-og	bog	cog	dog	fog
	hog	jog	log	
-ob	Bob	cob	gob	job
	lob	mob	rob	sob
-od	cod	God	nod	odd
	pod	rod	sod	Todd
-off	off			
-oll	doll	loll		
-om	mom	pom	Tom	
-on	con	Don	Jon	Ron
-op	bop	cop	hop	lop
	mop	pop	sop	top
-ot	cot	dot	Dot	got
	hot	jot	lot	pot	rot
	tot			
-ox	box	fox	lox	pox

Lesson 11
Words ending in -*ck*, plus those ending in -*all*[1]

-ack	back	hack	Jack	lack
	Mack	pack	quack	rack
	sack	stack	tack	Zack
-eck	deck	neck	peck	
-ick	Dick	kick	lick	Nick
	pick	quick	Rick	sick
	tick	wick		
-ock	cock	dock	lock	mock
	rock	sock	tock	
-uck	buck	duck	luck	muck
	puck	suck	tuck	
-all	all	ball	call	fall
	gall	hall	mall	small
	tall	wall		

---

[1] Remember that, until they are familiar with the way these combinations work, for some children it can be helpful to underline true digraphs (letter-combinations like *qu*, *ck*, and so forth, that sound different together than one would expect them to sound if they were apart). The underline alerts the reader to some of the slightly odd usages.

Lesson 12
Words beginning with *bl-, cl-, fl-,* and *gl-*[1]

bl-	black	bland	blast	bled
	bless	blip	bliss	block
	blond	blot	bluff	
cl-	clack	clad	clam	clan
	clap	clef	Clem	click
	cliff	clip	clock	clod
	clog	club	cluck	
fl-	flack	flag	flap	flat
	fleck	fled	flick	flint
	flip	flit	flock	flog
	flop	floss	flub	fluff
gl-	glad	gland	glass	glasses
	Glen	glib	glom	glop
	gloss	glug	glum	glut

---

[1] **Teaching hint:** If your children have difficulty with these multi-consonant words, cover the first letter and have them read the rest. "What is this word? Yes: *lack*. First we say /b/, and then we say /lack/. We we say /b/, then we say /lack/. /black/. Now it is your turn . . ."

Lesson 13

Words beginning with *pl-, sk-,* and *sl-,*
and those ending with *-nk* [1]

pl-	plan	plod	plop	plot
	pluck	plug	plum	plus
sk-	skid	skiff	skill	skim
	skin	skip	skit	skull
sl-	slab	slack	slam	slap
	slat	sled	slick	slid
	slim	slip	slit	slob
	slop	slot	slug	slum
-nk	blink	clink	drink	ink
	kink	link	mink	pink
	rink	sink	slink	stink
	think	wink	bonk	conk
	honk	bunk	clunk	dunk
	flunk	hunk	junk	punk
	plunk	sunk	skunk	stunk

[1] Please feel no pressure to have your children read all these words. We simply know that some children take pleasure in reading lots of words. Others may struggle, but they enjoy the slightly "naughty" words like *slop, slug, stink* and *stunk*. Please use these lists as you think is best. (And remember: you can have your kids read down the columns as well as across!)

Lesson 14
Words beginning with *cr-, dr-,* and *gr-*[1]

cr-	crab	crack	crag	cram
	crass	crib	crick	crock
	crop	cross	crud	
dr-	drab	drag	dreg	dress
	drill	drink	drip	drop
	drug	drum	drunk	
gr-	grab	grad	gram	gran
	grand	grass	Greg	grid
	grill	grim	grin	grip
	grit	grog	grub	gruff

---

[1] **Teaching hint:** If your children have difficulty with the vowel sounds, have them say the vowels by themselves first and then sound out the entire word.

Lesson 15

Words beginning with *br-*, *fr-*, *pr-*, and *tr-*

br-	Brad	brag	bran	brass
	brat	bred	brick	brig
	brim	bring		

fr-	Fran	frat	Fred	fret
	frill	frizz	frock	frog

pr-	pram	prep	press	prick
	prim	prod	prom	prop

tr-	track	tram	trap	trek
	tress	trick	trill	trim
	trip	trod	trot	truck

Lesson 16

Words beginning with *sc-, sm-, sn-,* and *sp-*

sc-	scab	scam	scan	scat
	scoff	Scott	scuff	scum
sm-	smack	smell	smock	smog
sn-	snack	snag	snap	sniff
	snip	snob	snub	snuck
	snuff	snug		
sp-	spam	span	spat	speck
	sped	spell	spent	Spot
	spud	spun		

Lesson 17
Words beginning with *st-*, *sw*, and *tw-*

st- stab   stack   staff   stag

stamp   Stan   stem   step

stick   stiff   still   stock

stop   stub   stuck   stud

stuff   stun

sw- swag   swam   swell   swig

swill   swim   Swiss

tw- twig   twill   twin   twit

Lesson 18
Words beginning with *qu-* and *squ-*[1]

qu- quack   quell   quest   quick

quid   quill   quip   quit

quiz

squ- squid   squint

---

[1] Remember to underline the *qu* to help your children see that the two letters make one sound.

Lesson 19
Words ending with *-mp, -sk,* and *-st*

-mp	camp	clamp	cramp	damp
	lamp	ramp	stamp	tramp
	blimp	limp	wimp	clomp
	romp	stomp	bump	clump
	dump	hump	jump	lump
	pump	plump	slump	stump
-sk	ask	cask	flask	mask
	task	desk	disk	risk
	dusk	husk	musk	tusk
-st	blast	cast	fast	last
	past	vast	best	jest
	nest	pest	quest	rest
	test	vest	zest	fist
	list	mist	twist	frost
	lost	crust	dust	gust
	just	must	rust	trust

Lesson 20
Words ending with *-ft, -fts, -lt, -lts, -nt*, and *-nts*

-ft	aft	craft	draft	graft
	raft	waft	left	drift
	gift	lift	sift	swift
	loft	soft	tuft	
-lt	belt	felt	melt	pelt
	smelt	welt	hilt	jilt
	kilt	lilt	silt	stilt
	tilt	wilt	cult	
-nt	ant	can't	Grant	pant
	plant	rant	slant	bent
	dent	lent	pent	rent
	sent	spent	tent	vent
	went	flint	glint	hint
	lint	mint	print	stint
	blunt	brunt	grunt	hunt
	punt	runt	stunt	

Lesson 21
Words ending with *-lf, -lk, -lp*, and *-nd*

-lf	elf	self	golf	Rolf
	gulf			
-lk	elk	milk	silk	bulk
	hulk	sulk	skulk	
-lp	Alps	scalp	help	kelp
	whelp	yelp	gulp	pulp
-nd	and	band	bland	brand
	gland	grand	hand	land
	sand	stand	bend	blend
	fend	lend	mend	rend
	send	spend	tend	trend
	wend	bond	blond	fond
	fund			

Lesson 22
Words ending with *-pt*

-pt   apt   crept   kept   slept

           swept   wept   adapt   adept

           adopt

Lesson 23
Single-syllable words ending with -e, -i, -o, and -y

-e	be	bee	fee	he
	me	see	tee	tree
	we	ye		
-i	hi	bi[1]	di	pi[2]
-o	Bo	go	Jo	lo
	Mo	no	so	yo-yo
-y	by	cry	dry	fly
	fry	my	ply	pry
	sky	sly	spy	spry
	sty	try	why	
-y	any			

---

[1] You may want to explain that *bi-* and *di-* are prefixes that your child will often run across in other words. For example: *bi* can be found in such words as *bicycle, bi-focals, biennial, bicentennial, bi-level, bilateral, binary*. . . . "What do you think *bi* means?" you may ask. (It means—or refers to—two: two-wheeled vehicle (*bicycle*), two-part glasses (*bi-focals*), every two months (*bimonthly*); every two years (*biennially*), etc. And *di* can be found in words like *diatomic* (composed of two atoms), *dichromatic* (having two possible colors), *dicotyledon* (having two seed-leaves), etc. We can see that *bi-* and *di-* have the same basic meanings. *Bi-* is from the Latin; *di-* is from Greek. For some reason, most of the *di-* words are used in the sciences.

[2] *Pi* stands on its own. It refers to a ratio: the circumference of a circle (how far it is around) divided by its diameter (how far it is across). No matter how big or small the circle, the ratio of circumference to diameter is always the same: 3.14159 . . .

Lesson 24
Long-vowel words with silent *e*'s, Part I[1]

a-e	ate	bade	blame	cane
	dame	fade	fate	gale
	glade	hate	Jane	lake
	made	mane	mate	name
	pale	pane	rake	rate
	safe	same	scare	stare
	tape	vane	wade	wake
-e-e	here	mere	Pete	
-ee-	beep	deed	feel	heed
	Jeep®	keel	peek	peep
	queen	reed	seek	seem
	seen	sees	trees	weed
i-e	bike	dine	fine	hide
	kite	life	like	lime

---

[1] Long vowels "say their names." The most common way to create a long vowel is to place an *e* after a vowel. This also works if the *e* comes at the end of the word and you put a consonant between the *e* and the vowel If there is only one consonant in front of the *e*, then whatever vowel is in front of that consonant will say its name.

    Examples: mad → made; pet → Pete; fin → fine; hop → hope; cub → cube

    To help your children understand this principle, have them go through the lists of long-vowel words that end with a silent *e* and see how many legitimate short-vowel words they can make simply by removing the final *e*. We have included, in Appendix 3, a list of those we discovered for Lesson 24.

	mile	mine	pile	pine
	prime	ride	ripe	side
	slide	time	wine	wife
-ie	die	lie	pie	tie
o-e	bone	code	cope	doze
	home	hope	lope	mope
	node	nose	note	poke
	pole	pope	robe	rode
	slope	tone	tote	woke
-oe	doe	foe	hoe	Joe
	toe	woe		
u-e[1]	cube	cute	fume	huge
	mule	use	duke	jute
	Luke	plume	tube	tune
-ue	cue	due	Sue	sue
	hue	rue		

[1] In the *u*-[consonant]-*e* words, pay attention to how one set of words has *u* truly "say" its name (with the full glide from the /ee/ to /oo/ sound). In the others, you never hear the sharp /ee/ sound. Listen carefully, for example, to the difference in pronunciation of the *u* in, say, the words *cute* and *dude* or *hue* and *Sue*.

Lesson 25
Long-vowel words with silent *e*'s, Part II

a-e	ace	age[1]	bane	bare
	base	cage	came	care
	cave	face	fake	gale
	gate	hare	haze	jade
	Jane	lace	lane	make
	maze	pace	page	race
	rare	sage	sale	tame
	tape	vale	wage	wave
-ee-	deep	feed	heel	keep
	meek	need	peel	reek
	seed	teen	week	weep
i-e	bite	dice	dime	dire
	fine	fire	hire	hive
	kite	lice	line	mice
	Mike	mime	mire	nice
	pine	pipe	rice	ride

[1] Though the letter *g* is not perfectly regular when followed by *e, i,* or *y* when it is at the beginning of a word, it is very regular when it is in the middle or toward the end. Notice how many soft *g*'s there are at the end of words that end in *-ge*!

	rile	size	tile	tire
	wine	wipe	wire	wise
-ie-	dies	lies	pies	ties
o-e	bore	core	cove	dome
	hole	hose	mole	more
	pore	role	rope	rose
	sore	vote	woke	wore
-oe	foes	hoes	toes	woes
u-e	cure	fuse	mute	pure
	dune	June	rude	rule

45

Lesson 26
Long-vowel words with silent *e*'s, Part III

a-e	blade	blare	blaze	brace
	brake	brave	crane	crave
	craze	drape	flake	flare
	frame	glare	glaze	grade
	grave	graze	plane	plate
	quake	scare	skate	slate
	slave	space	spare	square
	stale	stare	state	trade
-e-e	Steve	these		
-ee-	breed	breeze	greed	green
	squeeze	steel	wheel	wheeze
i-e	bride	Clive	crime	drive
	glide	grime	gripe	price
	pride	prize	quite	slice
	slide	slime	smile	spice
	spike	spine	splice	squire
	strike	strive	swine	swipe

	tribe	trike	trite	twice
	twine	wives	while	white
-ie-	cries	dries	flies	tries
o-e	broke	clone	drone	drove
	froze	grove	probe	prone
	quote	scone	scope	score
	slope	smoke	smote	snore
	spoke	stole	stone	store
	stove	stroke	swore	those
u-e	Bruce	brute	crude	flute
	plume	prune		
-ue	blue	clue	glue	true

Lesson 27
The *sh* digraph[1]

sh-			
shack	shade	shake	shall
shame	shape	share	shave
she	shed	shelf	shell
sheep	sheet	shift	shin
shine	ship	shock	shone
shop	shore	shot	shun
shut	shy	shred	shrill
shrine	shrink	shrub	shrug

-sh			
cash	clash	crash	dash
flash	gash	hash	mash
rash	sash	splash	trash
flesh	fresh	mesh	dish
fish	wish	Josh	posh
slosh	gush	blush	brush
crush	flush	hush	lush
mush	plush	rush	slush

[1] Remember: it may help to underline the *sh* to alert your children that the two letters make one sound. *Digraph* means "two-[symbol] writing." So it refers to a sound symbolized by a two-letter combination.

Lesson 28
The *wh* and *th* digraphs (vocalized and unvocalized)[1]

th- (unvocalized)	Thad	thrash	three	thick
	thin	thrill	thorn	throb
	throne	thud	thug	
th- (vocalized)	than	that	the	them
	then	there	these	they
	this	those	thus	thy
-th (unvocalized)	bath	math	path	Seth
	moth	smith	broth	cloth
	froth	sloth	truth	with
-th (vocalized)	bathe	lathe	lithe	tithe
wh-	whack	whale	wham	whap
	what	when	where	whiff
	while	whim	whine	whip
	white	whiz	who	whole
	whom	whose	why	

---

[1] Hold your hand to your neck just below your jaw while you say the *th* in *Thad* and *than*. Your vocal chords vibrate ("vocalize") with the *th* in *than*, but not with *Thad*!

Lesson 29
The *ch* digraph and *tch* blend

ch-	chaff	champ	chant	chap
	chat	check	cheek	cheer
	cheese	chess	chest	chick
	chill	chimp	chin	chink
	Chip	chock	chop	chore
	Chuck	chug	chum	chump
-ch	branch	bench	wench	cinch
	finch	inch	pinch	rich
	which	bunch	brunch	crunch
	French	lunch	much	munch
	punch	quench	such	scrunch
-tch	batch	catch	hatch	latch
	match	patch	scratch	snatch
	fetch	ditch	pitch	stitch
	clutch	Dutch		

Lesson 30

Words ending in *-ang, -ing, -ong*, or *-ung*

-ang	bang	clang	fang	gang
	hang	pang	rang	sang
	slang	sprang		
-ing	bring	cling	ding	fling
	king	Ming	ping	ring
	sing	sling	spring	sting
	string	thing	wing	
-ong	bong	gong	Hong	Kong
	long	pong	prong	song
	strong	thongs	tongs	throng
-ung	clung	dung	flung	gung-ho
	hung	lung	rung	sung
	sprung	stung		

Lesson 31
Suffixes, Part I (-*ing*)[1]

brand/ing	hand/ing	standing
granting	planting	slanting
wanting	passing	casting
taxing	waxing	billing
filling	fussing	mussing
hissing	kissing	pecking
kicking	licking	sticking

* * *

docking	locking	bucking
chucking	tucking	calling
falling	blasting	blocking
bluffing	clicking	stacking
inking	sinking	honking
bunking	cracking	crossing

* * *

dressing	drilling	scuffing

[1] Cover the suffix and have your children read the root word by itself . . . and then again with the suffix

smacking	smelling	snacking
sniffing	stuffing	camping
stamping	tramping	crimping
limping	romping	bumping
jumping	lumping	masking

* * *

risking	blasting	jesting
nesting	listing	twisting
frosting	busting	crafting
drafting	drifting	lifting
bending	blending	mending

* * *

sending	tending	glinting
grunting	hunting	golfing
milking	sulking	scalping
helping	yelping	gulping
bonding	crying	flying
frying	spying	trying

Lesson 32
The vowel digraphs: *ea* and *ee*[1]

-ee-	beef	beer	breeze	cheek
	cheese	creep	deem	feed
	feel	flee	free	freeze
	geese	greed	heed	heel
	jeer	keen	peek	queen
	screen	seed	sleeve	sneer
	street	teen	teepee	three
	veer	weed	week	wheeze
-ea-	each	ear	ease	beach
	bean	bleak	cheat	cleave
	dream	freak	heat	heave
	jeans	leap	lease	peak
	plead	please	reap	rear
	scream	sleaze	streak	shear
	team	tease	treat	veal
	wean	wheat	year	yeast

[1] Two vowels together, especially *ai, ay, ea, ee, oa* and *ow*, normally form a single sound: the long sound of the first vowel. (Two potential useful mnemonics for this phenomenon: "When two vowels go walking, the first one does the talking." Or, "When two vowels meet, the first one says its name.")

Lesson 33
The vowel digraphs: *ai* and *ay*

-ai-	bail	chain	chair	claim
	drain	fail	faint	fair
	flail	flair	frail	gain
	gait	grail	grain	hail
	jail	mail	nail	pail
	pain	paint	pair	plain
	quail	quaint	rail	rain
	raise	sail	slain	snail
	Spain	sprain	stain	stair
	strain	tail	trail	train
	trait	vain	waif	wait
-ay	bay	clay	day	fray
	gray	hay	lay	May
	nay	pay	play	pray
	Ray	say	slay	spray
	stay	stray	tray	way

Lesson 34
The vowel digraphs: *oa* and *ow*

-oa-	oaf	oak	oar	oat
	boar	boat	bloat	coal
	coat	coax	cloak	croak
	float	goad	goal	goat
	gloat	groan	hoax	Joan
	load	loaf	loan	moan
	moat	poach	roach	road
	roam	soak	soap	soar
	shoal	toad	whoa	
-ow	owe	bow	bowl	blow
	crow	flow	glow	grow
	low	mow	row	sow
	show	slow	snow	stow
	tow			

Lesson 35
Compound words[1]

Now we move from reading basic, one-syllable words, to recognizing and reading words of two syllables or more. When a word is made of two shorter words, it is called a *compound* word. Can your children see and say the two separate words?

ant/hill	air/plane	backfire
baseball	bedtime	campfire
catfish	classmate	cupcake
daytime	drumstick	dustpan
earring	earwax	fireman
fishpond	flagpole	gunfire
hairbrush	hamstring	handbag
hangman	houseboat	inside
kidnap	kingpin	lampshade
livestock	myself	nitpick
nosecone	nosegear	nothing
oatmeal	outfit	paintbrush
pancake	peanut	pickax
racetrack	railroad	rosebud

---

[1] If your children have difficulty "seeing" the two halves of these words, you can show where they divide by using a colored pen. Or underline the first "half" of the word to show the two parts.

rowboat	sailboat	sandbox
scarecrow	seagull	skyline
snowman	swingset	teapot
tidbit	tomcat	topsail
towtruck	trashcan	update
upset	whiplash	windmill
wingtip	wishbone	within

* * *

age/less[1]	back/less	beltless
blameless	boneless	careless
dateless	dentless	dustless
faceless	gutless	hatless
helpless	homeless	hopeless
endless	nameless	reckless
scoreless	smokeless	spineless
stateless	timeless	tireless
tubeless	useless	wireless

---

[1] Here is a large collection of compounds composed of a root plus the suffix/additional word *less*.

Lesson 36
Suffixes, Part II (*-ing, -ful, -ed, -en, -est, -ness, -ly, -able*)[1]

-ing

bail/ing	bleat/ing	chaining
cheating	cleaning	cloaking
crowing	dealing	draining
dreaming	eating	failing
fearing	feeding	floating
flowing	freeing	gaining
gleaning	goading	graying
healing	heeding	jeering
keeping	laying	leaping
leering	loading	meaning
moaning	mowing	nearing
needing	painting	peeling
peeping	pinching	playing
poaching	praying	preening
railing	roaming	rowing

---

[1] Suffixes *-ing, -ful, -ed, -en, -est, -ness, -ly, -able*.
Have your student pick out and read the root word by itself . . . and then again together with the suffix.
Notice that, in the case of words ending in *-ed*, we are concentrating only on words that end with a *d* or a *t* because it is only with these words that the *-ed* adds a syllable. With all other words, the suffix *-ed* changes the pronunciation and meaning of the word but does not actually add a second syllable. Just a few examples: **blinked, bluffed, camped, drilled, fussed, jumped, licked, pecked, romped, stocked, yelled,** and **zonked**

	sailing	saying	screaming
	sealing	seeking	showing
	sneaking	sneering	soaring
	speaking	spearing	speeding
	staining	straining	streaking
	streaming	tailing	towing
	trailing	training	waiting
-ful	care/ful	cup/ful	fateful
	grateful	handful	hateful
	hopeful	painful	wakeful
	helpful	restful	tearful
	prideful	wishful	hopeful
	thankful	trustful	willful
-ed	band/ed	belt/ed	blasted
	busted	crafted	dented
	drafted	frosted	granted
	hinted	hunted	lasted
	lifted	melted	misted

	panted	printed	punted
	ranted	rested	rusted
	sanded	sifted	slanted
	squinted	tested	tilted
	trusted	vented	wilted
-en	fall/en	flaxen	golden
-est	black/est	blond/est	bluntest
	dampest	fastest	fondest
	grandest	gruffest	plumpest
	quickest	sickest	softest
	stiffest	tallest	vastest
-ness	aptness	baseness	blackness
	blueness	braveness	crudeness
	dimness	drabness	dryness
	fatness	fondness	gladness
	graveness	grimness	gruffness
	illness	lameness	laxness
	likeness	madness	paleness
	quickness	redness	ripeness

	rudeness	sadness	sameness
	sickness	slyness	smugness
	staleness	stiffness	tallness
	tameness	trimness	wetness
-ly	agelessly	badly	blamelessly
	carefully	endlessly	fatefully
	gratefully	gutlessly	hatefully
	helpfully	hopefully	hopelessly
	madly	merely	painlessly
	pridefully	recklessly	sadly
	tearfully	thankfully	timelessly
	tunefully	trustfully	usefully
	vastly	wakefully	wishfully
-able	catchable	dentable	employable
	gatherable	kissable	linkable
	mendable	passable	readable
	sendable	tellable	walkable

Lesson 37
Dividing two-syllable words, Part I[1]

ab/bot	ap/peal	appear
attack	attend	attic
ballad	ballast	balloon
ballot	batter	bellow
bitter	blossom	bonnet
bottom	butter	button
channel	chatter	clatter
common	comment	connect
cotton	dinner	dollop
effect	fellow	fetter
Finnish	flutter	gallon
gallop	gossip	hammer
hammock	happen	hello
Kenneth	kitten	ladder
latter	lesson	letter

---

[1] When a word has two syllables—which means it has two vowels that you can hear; and when the two vowels are separated by a double consonant (two copies of the same consonant), then the word breaks between the two consonants. The first syllable is "closed" (meaning it ends with a consonant), and its vowel is short. The second syllable begins with the second copy of the consonant with which the first syllable ends.

litter	mallet	matter
mellow	mitten	muffin
mutter	mutton	paddock
patter	pepper	petted[1]
pitter	platter	puppet
quitter	rabbit	ribbon
robber	rubber	rubbish
scallop	setting	shatter
simmer	sitter	slipper
sonnet	sudden	summer
supper	tennis	titter
traffic	tunnel	wedding
wetter	yellow	zipper

---

[1] Why do *petted, petting, wedded* and *wedding* fit under the rule for this lesson, while *butted, butting* and *pulling* do not? Put another way: why should *petted* be divided *pet-ted*, *wedded* as *wed-ded*, *petting* as *pet-ting* and *wedding* as *wed-ding*, while *butted* is divided *butt-ed*, *butting* as *butt-ing*, and *pulling* as *pull-ing*?

When you have a word that ends in a single consonant, and you want to add a suffix that begins with a vowel (*-ing* or *-ed*), you have to double the final consonant and add the suffix. And in each case, the additional "final consonant" joins with the suffix to form the final syllable of the new word.

But both *t*'s in *butted*, both *t*'s in *butting*, and both *l*'s in *pulling* are natural parts of their roots. No one had to add a second consonant in order to form these words. These single-syllable root words come with two consonants. You don't break apart the original root syllable when you add a suffix.

Lesson 38
Dividing two-syllable words, Part II[1]

ab/sent	ad/mit	bandit
basket	candid	compact
conduct	consent	contact
content	contest	costume
crumpet	dentist	disgust
dispatch	enforce	engage[2]
engulf	enlist	enrich
escape	filter	forget
goblet	hamper	impact
index	intent	kidnap
largest	magnet	mailman
napkin	nonsense	number
padlock	perform	picnic
plastic	presto	problem
public	publish	random

---

[1] Again, all first syllables are closed and the vowels, therefore, are short!

[2] Remember! The letters *c* and *g* become "soft" when they are followed by *i, e,* and (usually) *y*. Now that we are dealing with two-syllable words, we will be running into this phenomenon much more frequently than we have up to this point.

sandal	scamper	seldom
selfish	signal	sister
splinter	suspect	tablet
tamper	temper	tinsel
thunder	triplet	trumpet
under	unpack	until
velvet	window	winter
wonder		

Lesson 39
"Open" and "closed" syllables[1]

Open/Long

acorn	basic	bonus
David	final	focus
hotel	human	ion
Joseph	local	major
minor	navy	oral
putrid	rotate	sacred
soda[2]	tiger	Tony
unit	vacant	vinyl
zebra		

Closed/Short

append	banish	confide
damsel	effect	factory
gamble	humble	jumble

---

[1] At this point, except for the fact that we have the opportunity to practice reading words with which we are unfamiliar, the "rules" we are studying have little if anything to do with reading. They may, occasionally, help wth spelling. From the perspective of trying to help your children read words they don't know, the best advice we can give is to try sounding them out with short and then long vowels. If the word doesn't sound right with a short vowel, then try pronouncing it with a long vowel.

From a "rules" perspective: when a syllable ends with a vowel, the syllable is "open" and the vowel is almost always long. When a syllable ends with a consonant, it is "closed" and its vowel is normally short.

[2] Here (-*da*) we have one of those rare "open" syllables that has a short vowel!

linseed	monster	Nancy
object	pontoon	quit
riddle	sincere	tinsel
under		

Extra Credit: Three-Syllable Words

cucumber	eternal	gorilla
koala	nuclear	wilderness
operate		

Lesson 40
Dividing two-syllable words, Part III[1]

a/gent	ba/con	basic
before	begin	below
broken	chosen	clover
crocus	decide	demand
direct	diver	emerge
erase	evil	evoke
focus	frozen	hotel
human	humid	item
local	major	minor
minus	motel	music
omit	open	paper
pilot	Polish[2]	polite
predate	prepare	pretax
prevent	proceed	protect

[1] Here our task is to decide where the boundary is between the two syllables. You may *mark* the boundaries (as we have with the first two words), or simply "spell them out loud."

For the purposes of spelling: if a word begins with a long vowel, you know it is part of an open syllable—except and unless the word is formed from a long-voweled root to which a suffix has been added. Long-voweled roots to which suffixes have been added do not follow this rule. For example: the word *biting* is not formed from an open syllable *bi* plus a closed syllable *ting*. It is composed of its "root" (*bite*) and its suffix (*ing*). It is formed by taking the word *bite*, deleting the final *e,* and adding *-ing*.

[2] Notice how important the syllable break becomes in a word like *Polish*. *Po-lish* is very different from *pol-ish* (which we will study in our next lesson)!

recent	remark	report
robot	silent	silo
skated	spoken	stated
student	stupid	taken
tiger	total	tulip
unite	united	zero

Lesson 41
Dividing two-syllable words, Part IV

Ad/am	cab/in	camel
comic	closet	credit
debit	Denver	devil
dragon	drivel	driven
exam	finish	gavel
given	gravel	Kevin
lemon	level	limit
madam	medal	metal
panel	pedal	planet
polish	prison	robin
salad	seven	sever
shovel	snivel	solid
timid	travel	vanish
wagon		

Lesson 42
Two-syllable words ending with -y[1]

ba/by	bat/ty	belly
buggy	bunny	candy
catty	clumsy	crazy
crummy	dandy	dolly
fatty	fifty	forty
funny	gravy	guppy
handy	happy	ivy
jelly	jolly	kitty
lazy	nasty	navy
plenty	pony	puppy
ratty	runny	seventy
silly	sixty	skinny
sunny	tinny	tiny
twenty	windy	

[1] Note that 1) -y words formed from a root that has had a -y suffix added to it normally divide, as most root-suffix words do, between the root and the suffix. (Thus, for example, *crusty, dumpy, dusty, grassy,* etc., all divide between their roots and the ending -y. However, a few words, such as *crazy* and *lazy*, do not seem to follow this rule. (There is a word *crazed*, and there is a word *laze*. I cannot account for why these would break as *cra-zy* and *la-zy*.)

2) The rules of "open" and "closed" syllables still apply! Your child can tell how *tiny* and *tinny* ought to be spelled (for example) based on their pronunciations. A long vowel (the *i* in *tiny*) requires an open syllable. *Tiny* must be spelled with only a single *n*. . . .

Lesson 43
Two-syllable words ending with -le[1]

able	amble	ample
apple	battle	beetle
bobble	bottle	bramble
bridle	bubble	bumble
bundle	cable	candle
cattle	crackle[2]	cradle
crinkle	cripple	crumble
cuddle	dapple	dimple
duffle	example	fable
fickle	fiddle	freckle
gamble	gobble	grapple
grumble	handle	hobble
huddle	humble	jiggle
jungle	kettle	ladle

---

[1] Once more you should stress the value of these kinds of "rules" to help your child's spelling. For instance, why must *bobble, cobble, hobble* and *wobble* be spelled with two *b*'s? (Because if they had only one, the first syllable in each case would be open, and the *o* would be long. . . .)

[2] Syllabification rules take precedence over what we might otherwise consider "rules" of meaning or phonics. The *ck* letter combination seems, normally, as if it should be considered as a single letter: you should never split the *c* from the *k*. But when it comes to syllables, you do! Therefore the first syllable in *crackle* is closed (*crac*) and the second syllable is composed of *-le* and its preceding consonant: *kle: crac-kle*. Similarly with *pickle* and *speckle*.

little	mantle	middle
muddle	muffle	mumble
needle	nibble	nimble
paddle	pickle	puddle
raffle	rattle	riddle
ripple	rubble	ruffle
rumble	saddle	sample
scramble	scuffle	settle
simple	snuggle	speckle
stable	steeple	struggle
stubble	stumble	table
temple	thimble	tickle
tingle	topple	tumble
twinkle	wobble	

Lesson 44
Words ending with *-alk, -all*, or *-alm*

all	alms	balk	ball
balm	chalk	call	calm
fall	gall	hall	mall
pall	palm	qualm	small
squall	stalk	stall	talk
tall	enthrall	walk	wall

Lesson 45
Words ending with *-old, -olt*, and *-oll*

bold	bolt	boll[1]	cold
colt	dolt	fold	gold
hold	jolt	mold	molt
old	poll[2]	roll	scold
sold	stroll	told	toll
troll			

---

[1] The seed-bearing portion of some plants: cotton and flax are the most common plants with bolls.

[2] *Poll* means "head." It is the word from which we got our word for "taking a poll" and "poll tax."

Lesson 46
Words ending in *-ild* and *-ind*

bind	blind	child	find
grind	hind	kind	mild
mind	rind	wild	wind[1]

---

[1] This is the one exception that can have either a short or *a* long *i*. You determine which it is based on the context.

Lesson 47

Review: *qu*[1]

acquaint	acquire	acquit
equal	equine[2]	equip
liquid	quack	quality
qualm	quandary	quarrel
quart	queen	quench
quest	quibble	quick
quickly	quicksand	quiet
quietly	quill	quilted
quilting	quintet	quintuplets
quit	quite	quiver
quiz	quote	sequel
square	squash	squat
squeak	squeal	squeeze
squid	squish	squire

---

[1] This lesson focuses on the common *qu* combinations that sound /kw/. Very rarely the *u* after *q* is silent. In these cases, *qu* says /k/ as in *liquor, milquetoast, quiche,* and *torque*. It appears that all of these words come from French.

[2] *Equine*: having to do with horses.

Lesson 48
Two-syllable words ending with -*ey* [1]

chimney	donkey	hockey	honey
jockey	kidney	money	monkey
pokey	pulley	smokey	Stanley
trolley	valley	volley	

---

[1] Two-syllable words ending in -*ey* conclude with the long *e* sound (/ee/). One-syllable words that end with -*ey* usually have the long *a* sound: *grey, hey, prey, whey*. *Key* is the only one-syllable -*ey* word I can think of that breaks this rule.

Lesson 49
Words with -ar

ar
(short o-r)

arch	archer	are
ark	arm	armor
Arnold	artist	bar
barge	bark	barn
car	card	cart
char	charm	collar
dark	dart	far
farm	garden	hard
hark	harp	jar
lard	large	leotard
march	mark	market
parcel	park	part
party	scar	scarf
shark	snarf	snarl
spar	spark	sparkle

	star	tar	tardy
	target	varnish	yarn
ar[1] (schwa-*r*)	beggar	cellar	collar
	coward	custard	dollar
	nuclear	peculiar	singular
	standard	vinegar	wizard
-ar-[2] (long *o-r*)	swarm	toward	war
	warm	warn	wart

* * *

From here on out, you should consider the "Lessons" more in the way of awareness- builders than subject matter your child needs to master. As I suggested in the note on the bottom of page 67 in Lesson 39, by the time they have gotten to this point, most readers can figure out the appropriate pronunciation from the contextual meaning. We encourage you to permit your child the freedom to pursue this kind of "discovery" method of reading.

So why do we include the following lessons? Because they can help your child feel that s/he has "permission" to mentally try alternative pronunciations ("It could be ____, but it might also be ____. Which makes more sense?")

* * *

---

[1] The *schwa* is similar to a very short *e*—so short, you almost can't hear it.
[2] The long *o-r* sound, it seems, is found only when the *ar* combination follows a *w*.

Lesson 50
-or- words

or
(long o-r)

adorn	assorted	born
chortle	cork	corner
for	forbid	forget
fork	forlorn	hornet
horse	Lord	morsel
mortal	orphan	porch
pork	record	report
resort	short	sorbet
sport	storm	torch
thorn	torn	tort
vortex	worn	York

or
(schwa-*r*)

actor	attorney	comfort
counselor	doctor	junior
razor	record	stubborn
word	work	world
worm	worry	worship
worth		

Lesson 51
-er-, -ir-, and -ur- words[1]

after	berm	birth	bitter
burn	burr	chirp	church
curl	dirt	fern	fir
first	furl	furnish	girl
gurney	her	hurl	hurt
irk	jerk	jury	kernel
Kurds	lurch	mercy	mermaid
mirth	murder	nerd	nurse
operate	percent	perch	perfect
purse	rural	seller	serpent
skirt	squirt	stir	tern
third	Thursday	turf	turn
urchin	urn	Vern	virtue

---

[1] Spelling help: the schwa-*r* sound is formed most commonly by the letter combination *er* (usually at the end of a word); the next most common spelling is *ir*. But as you have seen, *or* and and *ar* can make the sound as well.

Lesson 52

-igh- words

bright	delight	downright
fight	flight	fright
high	insight	light
lightning	might	nigh
night	plight	right
sigh	sight	sunlight
tight	tightrope	upright

Lesson 53
-oo- words

oo (short *oo*)			
	book	brook	cook
	crook	foot	forsook
	good	hood	hook
	look	nook	shook
	soot	stood	took
	wood		

oo (long *oo*)			
	aloof	boom	boon
	boot	broom	boost
	choose	coo	cool
	croon	food	fool
	gloom	goose	kangaroo
	lagoon	loom	mood
	moon	noon	platoon
	poodle	proof	raccoon
	rooster	shoot	soon
	soothe	spook	stool
	stoop	tool	tooth

Lesson 54
-*ea*- words

ea (short *e*)	abreast	bread	cleanliness
	dead	feather	head
	health	instead	lead[1]
	leather	meadow	measure
	thread	treasure	zealot
ea (schwa[-*r*])	dearth	early	earnest
	heard	hearse	learn
	pearl	search	yearn
ea (long *e*)	beach	breathe	clean
	dear	each	ear
	eat	flea	gear
	hear	lean	meat
	neat	peach	tear[2]
ea (long *a*)	break	great	pear
	steak	tear	wear
ea (short *o*[-*r*])	hearken	heart	hearth

---

[1] The metal.

[2] Only by context can you tell whether *tear* has to do with moisture from the eyes (*tear* with the sound of a long *e*) or destruction of fabric (*tear* with a long *a* sound).

Lesson 55
-ie- words

ie (long *e*)		
achieve	belief	believe
besiege	brief	brownie
cashier	chief	collie
field	fiend	fierce
frontier	genie	grief
grieve	movie	niece
piece	pierce	priest
relief	relieve	reverie
shield	tier	wield
yield		

ie (long *i*)		
die	fie	hie
lie	pie	tie
vie		

ie (short *e*)
friend

ie (short *i*)
mischief   sieve

Lesson 56
-oi- and *-oy-* words

oi	appoint	avoid	boil
	broil	choice	coil
	coin	doily	exploit
	foil	hoist	join
	joint	loin	moist
	noise	noisy	oil
	ointment	point	poise
	roil	sirloin	soil
	spoil	toil	voice
oi	choir		
oi	porpoise	tortoise	
oy	alloy	annoy	boy
	boycott	convoy	coy
	destroy	employ	joy
	loyal	oyster	royal
	soy	Troy	viceroy
	voyage		

Lesson 57
-ou- words[1]

ou
(/ow/)

about	account	bound
bout	cloud	clout
couch	count	devour
dour	flour	foul
found	grouch	hour
mouth	out	pouch
snout	announce	

ou
(short *u*)

callous	country	couple
cousin	double	dubious
envious	famous	nervous
pious	southern	strenuous
touch	trouble	young
zealous		

ou
(long *o*)

boulder	course	court
dough	four	gourd
mourn	pour	resource

---

[1] The long *oo* and schwa-*r* words are all from French!

	shoulder	soul	your
ou (long *oo*)	acoustic	boulevard	contour
	coupe	group	routine
	souvenir	through	tour
	troupe	youth	
ou (schwa)	adjourn	courage	flourish
	glamour	journal	nourish

Lesson 58
-ow- words

ow
(/ow/)

bow[1]	brow	brown
browse	clown	cow
cowl	crown	down
dowry	drown	flower
fowl	frown	gown
growl	how	howl
jowl	now	owl
plow	pow	powder
prowl	scowl	shower
towel	town	trowel
vow	wow	

ow
(long *o*)

arrow	bellow	below
borrow	bow	bowl
bowling	bungalow	crow
elbow	fellow	fellowship
flow	gallows	grow

[1] Another word whose pronunciation and meaning you can tell only if you read it in context—or you hear someone say it! Is it the front of a boat (or a symbolic gesture made by bending at the waist)? Or is it a weapon (or a type of knot)?

grown	know	known
low	mow	narrow
own	pillow	row
shadow	show	slow
sorrow	sparrow	stow
throw	thrown	tow

Lesson 59
-au- and *-aw-* words

au	audio	August	astronaut
	caught	clause	daughter
	exhaust	faucet	fault
	fraud	gauze	haul
	jaunt	launch	laundry
	naughty	Paul	sauce
	taught	vault	
au	laugh		
au	gauge		
au	beauty		
au	sauerkraut		
aw	awe	awful	awkward
	crawl	dawdle	flaw
	gawky	hawk	jaw
	lawn	paw	raw
	seesaw	shawl	squawk
	straw	thaw	yawn

Lesson 60

-eu-, -ew-, -ue-, and *-ui-* words

eu (long *oo*)	deuce	maneuver		neutral
eu (*y*-long *oo*)	eulogy	feud	neurotic	therapeutic
ew (long *oo*)	blew	chew	drew	ewe
	flew	grew	Jewish	jewel
	knew	new	renew	sewer
ew (*y*-long *oo*)	hew	mew	pew	skewer
	view	whew	yew	
ue (long *oo*)	accrue	avenue	blue	clue
	due	flue	fondue	glue
	revenue	rue	sue	true
ue (*y*-long *oo*)	argue	barbecue	continue	hue
	statue	value		
ui (long *oo*)	bruise	cruise	fruit	juice
	pursuit	sluice	suit	
ui (*y*-long *oo*)	nuisance			
ui (short *i*)	build	built	guild	guilt
ui (long *i*)	disguise	guide	guile	guise

Lesson 61
Review the soft *c* and *g*

ce	ace	brace	chance	dance
	force	grace	ice	lace
	mice	nice	office	price
	rice	trace	vice	wince
ci	accident	bracing	cigar	dancing
	Marcie	science	scissors	society
cy	bicycle	cycle	fancy	legacy
	Lucy	Marcy	Nancy	Quincy
	racy	spicy		
ge[1]	age	cage	danger	gem
	hinge	large	merge	Nigel
	orange	rage	sage	tinge
	urge	verge	village	wage
dge[2]	badger	bridge	budget	dodge
	edge	fidget	fudge	gadget

[1] When you hear a /j/ sound at the end of a word, it is always spelled -*ge*.
[2] If *ge* is to follow a short vowel, a *d* is inserted immediately before the *g* so that the silent *e* does not make the vowel long. However, notice that the word *judgment* has no *e* after the *g!*

95

	grudge	judge	lodge	midget
	nudge	ridge	sludge	widget
gi	agile	barging	caging	energize
	fragile	giant	imaging	logical
	margin	raging		
gy	analogy	biology	ecology	gym
	gypsy	liturgy	pudgy	strategy
dg	judgment			

Lesson 62
-er, -err-, -ar-, and *-arr-* words

er
coherent	Gerald	heritage
inherit	kerosene	numeric
peril	prosperity	sheriff
stationery	sterile	therapy
very		

err
berry	cherry	error
ferry	Jerry	merry
Perry	Terry	territory
terror		

ar
apparent	baron	Karen
Mary	parallel	parent
parity	stationary	tariff
vary	wary	

arr
arrow	barrel	barren
carrot	embarrass	garrison
Harry	marry	narrate
parrot		

Lesson 63
-ch- words[1]

ch
(/k/)

ache	anchor	chaos
character	chasm	chemical
chlorine	chord	chorus
Christ	chronology	echo
mocha	mechanic	scheme
school	stomach	technique

ch
(/sh/)

chamois	charade	chateau
Chevy	Chicago	chiffon
chivalry	cliché[2]	crochet
echelon	machine	Michigan
mustache	parachute	pistachio
ricochet	schwa	

[1] Notice that all the /k/ sound words are from the Greek where the letter *Chi* (pronounced with the /k/ and long i sounds) has been transliterated as *ch*. All the /sh/ sound words are from French!

[2] When you see the letter *e* with an acute accent over it (*é*), it is usually from a French or Spanish word. *É* is pronounced with a long *a* sound.

Lesson 64
-ci- and *-ti-* words

ci

ancient   commercial   conscience

crucial   delicious   emaciate

financial   judicious   official

politician   racial   social

spacious

ti

action   addition   caution

constitution   diction   dietitian

direction   education   imported

intention   negotiate   partial

partition   patience   ratio

recognition   section

Lesson 65
-du- and *-tu-* words

du   arduous   assiduous   educate

           gradual   graduate   incredulous

           individual   modulate   residual

tu   actual   adventure   culture

           denture   estuary   feature

           fortune   furniture   future

           habitual   literature   mature

           nature   picture   ritual

           sculpture   spiritual   suture

           temperature   virtue   vulture

di   cordial   soldier

Lesson 66

-*s*- can sound like /sh/ or /zh/ and -*ss*- can sound like /sh/

s or ss
(/sh/)

censure   erasure   fissure

insurance   issue   mission

passion   pressure   sensuous

surety   tissue   tonsure

s
(/zh/)

casual   closure   enclosure

exposure   leisure   measure

visual

Lesson 67
Silent *b, g, k, p,* and *w* words

-bt	debt	doubt	
mb	crumb	dumb	numb	plumber
gn	align	assign	benign	deign
	design	feign	foreign	gnash
	gnat	gnaw	gnu	impugn
	malign	reign	sign	sovereign
kn-	knack	knead	knee	kneel
	knew	knife	knit	knight
	knock	knoll	knot	know
pn-	pneumonia			
ps-	psalm	pseudonym	psychology	
wr-	wrangle	wrap	wrath	
	wreath	wreck	wren	
	wrench	wring	wrinkle	
	wrist	write	written	
	wrong	wrote	wry	

Lesson 68
-ph- and *-gh-* words

ph

alphabet	amphibian	dolphin
elephant	emphatic	geography
humph	hyphen	lymph
nephew	phone	photon
phrase	physician	sphere
telephone	zephyr	

-gh

cough	enough	laugh
rough	tough	

Five helpful spelling rules.

1. "*I* before *e* except after *c* or when making the long *a* sound."

   —Generally true, but there are several common exceptions. Valid examples: "*I* before *e*": *piece, achieve*; "except after *c*": *ceiling, perceive*; "or when making the long *a* sound": *veil, weigh*. Some of the common exceptions: *either, neither, seize, weird; heifer, leisure; feisty, height, kaleidoscope, stein. . . .*

2. "Use *k* before *e* and *i*; use *c* before other vowels."

   —Useful when wanting to spell words with the /k/ sound. (*Cat, keg, kit, cot, cut.*)

3. "Change *y* to *i* and add *-es* (or *-ed*)."

   —A helpful rule for nouns and verbs that end with a consonant-y combination.

4. "Drop the *e* and add *-ing*."

   —For use when adding the *-ing* suffix to words that end with a silent *e*.

5. "Double the final consonant before adding suffixes that begin with vowels (*-ing, -ed, -able,* etc.)."

   —Valid if a word ends with a single consonant and it either consists of a single, short-vowel syllable, or, if it has more than one syllable, the final, short-vowel syllable is accented. Valid examples: *fog — fogging/fogged*; *expel — expelling/expelled*. But beware of the exceptions! Words with accented syllables whose vowels are not short: *devour — devouring/devoured; look — looking/looked*. Words with no accent on the final, short-vowel syllable: *worship — worshiping/worshiped*.

Appendix 1:
Linguistics and Sound Formation

Linguists have noted that people around the world form sounds in certain common ways. As you study the chart below, try to form the sounds and feel carefully where you place your tongue, where you stop your breath, where the air goes while you speak, whether your vocal chords vibrate, and so forth. For instance, feel what your mouth, tongue, vocal chords, etc., do when you say "b" and compare that to what you do when you say "p." Compare those two sounds, then, to, say, "d" and "t." Can you feel the differences?

Please understand that I am no linguist. This is merely my *semi-educated* (probably not fully accurate) summary of a *portion* of the technical data a true linguist could give you. However, I have found that by studying these patterns, I am not only able to analyze why a person—child or adult—is having

	Vocalized	Non-Vocalized
Bi-Labial[1] Stop[2]	b	p
Bi-Labial Nasal[3]	m	
Bi-Labial Fricative[4]	w	"wh"
Labial-Dental Fricative	v	f
Lingual/Dental Non-Stopped	l	
Lingual[5]/Dental-ridge[6] Stop	d	t
Lingual/Dental-ridge Fricative	z	s
Lingual/Dental-ridge Fricative Stop	j	"ch"
Lingual/Dental-ridge Nasal	n	
Lingual/Palate Non-Stopped	r	
Glottal[7] Stop	g	hard c, k, q
Glottal Fricative	h	
Not Stopped	a, e, i, o, u	

[1]Labial: having to do with the lips. Bi-labial: having to do with two (i.e., both) lips.

[2]A "stop" occurs when there is a momentary complete closure of the air passage followed by a short, almost explosive release of air.

[3]Nasal: requiring air to pass through the nose.

[4]Fricative: pronounced by forcing the breath through a narrow slit formed at some point in the mouth.

[5]Lingual: having to do with the tongue.

[6]The dental-ridge is that part of the roof of your mouth immediately behind your front teeth.

[7]The glottis is the opening at the back of your throat.

difficulty pronouncing a certain sound, but also to understand why we pronounce certain words and certain letter-combinations as we do.

For example: a person who lisps usually does so because s/he tries to form the "s" sound as a lingual/*dental* rather than a lingual/dental-*ridge* fricative.

As for pronunciation, consider the final-s sound. Words ending in   -*ats, -aps, -ips* and -*its* all pronounce the *s* with the non-vocalized "s" sound. Words ending in -*ans, -ads, -ams, -ags, -abs, -als, -ids, -igs,* and -*ins* pronounce the *s* with the vocalized "z" sound. Can you figure out why? (Because the phonemes—or sounds—that immediately precede the *s* in the first case are non-vocalized (matching the non-vocalized "s" sound), while the phonemes that immediately precede the s in the second case are all vocalized—which matches the vocalized "z" sound.)

Does that make sense?

Here's another example of how and why a letter's sound changes. Think of the -*nk* combination: thi*nk*, tha*nk*sgiving, plu*nk*, and so forth. The *n* is not pronounced as a lingual/dental-ridge nasal sound, but as a glottal nasal—the "ng" sound. Why?

Think through how you pronounce the "k" sound. It is a non-vocalized glottal stop. Try to pronounce the word *thank*, for instance, using the normal "n" sound followed immediately by the "k" sound. Can you even do it? It is virtually impossible. The "n" will almost of necessity transform itself into an "ng" sound. . . .

Appendix 2:

Most Common Words in the English Language

According to Dr. Ruth Beechick,[1] the following words make up close to 25 percent of all words written in American English:

a, and, I, of, in, that, the, to, you

The following words make up the next 25 percent of all words written in American English:

all	**an**	**are**	**as**	**at**	**be**	**been**	**but**	**by**
dear	**for**	**from**	**had**	**has**	**have**	**he**	**her**	**his**
if	**is**	**it**	**me**	**my**	**not**	**on**	**one**	**or**
she	**so**	**there**	**they**	**this**	**very**	**was**	**we**	**were**
which	**will**	**with**	**would**	**your**				

If you can master these words, you have mastered nearly half of all the words you will ever write!

---

[1] Dr. Ruth Beechick, *A Strong Start in Language* (Pollock Pines, CA: Arrow Press, 1986), pp. 12-13. This is part of Dr. Beechick's *Three R's* series available from Sonlight Curriculum, Ltd.

Appendix 3:

Short-Vowel Words Created from Lesson 24

at	bad	blam	can	fad	fat	gal	glad	hat
Jan	mad	man	mat	pal	pan	rat	Sam	scar
star	tap							

her	pet

din	fin	hid	kit	pin	prim	rid	rip	Sid
slid	Tim	win						

cod	cop	hop	lop	mop	nod	not	pop	rob
rod	slop	[ton]	tot	wok[1]				

cub	cut	hug	us	jut	plum	tub	tun[2]

---

[1] Chinese cook pot. This is not the same as the word walk!

[2] Large cask.